Wendell Phillips

ON THE

"OLD SOUTH."

BOSTON, JUNE 14, 1876.

ORATION

DELIVERED IN THE

OLD SOUTH CHURCH

BY

WENDELL PHILLIPS,

JUNE 14, 1876.

LADIES AND GENTLEMEN: —

Why are we here to-day? Why should this relic, a hundred years old, stir your pulses to-day so keenly? We sometimes find a community or an individual with their hearts set on some old roof or great scene; and as we look on, it seems to us an exaggerated feeling, a fond conceit, an unfounded attachment, too emphatic value set on some ancient thing or spot which memory endears to them. But we have a right to-day — this year we have a right beyond all question, and with no possibility of exaggerating the importance of the hour — to ask the world itself to pause when this nation completes the first hundred years of its life. Because these forty millions of people have at last achieved what no race, no nation, no age hitherto has succeeded in doing. We have founded a Republic on the unlimited suffrage of the millions. We have actually worked out the problem that man, as God created him, may be trusted with self-government. We have shown the world that a Church without a Bishop, and a State without a King is an actual, real, everyday possibility. Look back over the history of the race, where will you find a chapter that precedes us in that achievement? Greece had her republics, but they were the republics of one freeman and ten slaves; and the battle of Marathon was fought by slaves unchained from the door-posts of their masters' houses. Italy had her republics: they were the republics of wealth and skill and family, limited and aristocratic. She had not risen to a sublime faith in man. Holland had her republic, the republic of guilds and landholders, trusting the helm of state to property and education. And all these which, at their best, held but a million or two within their narrow limits, have gone down in the ocean of time.

A hundred years ago, our fathers announced this sublime, and as it seemed then, foolhardy declaration, that God intended all men to be free and equal: all men, without restriction, without qualification, without limit. A hundred years have rolled away since that venturous declaration; and to-day, with a territory that joins ocean to ocean, with forty millions of people, with two wars behind her, with the sublime achievement of having grappled with the fearful disease that threatened her central life, and broken four millions of fetters, the great Republic, stronger than ever, launches into the second century of her existence. The history of the world has no such chapter, in its breadth, its depth, its significance, or its bearing on future history. Well may we claim that this centennial year is the baptism of the human race into a new hope for humanity. Are we not entitled then, coming with the sheaves of such a harvest in our hands, to say to the world, "Behold the blessing of God on our right faith in the human race!" Well, gentlemen, if that is sober prose, without one tittle of exaggeration, without one fond conceit borrowed from our kindred with the actors or from our birth in these streets,—if that is the sober record,—with how much pride, with what a thrill, with what tender and loyal reverence, may we not hunt up and cherish, and guard from change or desecration, the spot where this marvellous enterprise began—the roof under which its first councils were held—where the air still trembles and burns with Otis and Sam Adams?

Except the Holy City, is there any more memorable or

sacred place on the face of the earth than the cradle of such a change? Athens has her Acropolis, but the Greek can point to no such immediate and distinct results. Her influence passes into the web and woof of history, mixed with a score of other elements; and it needs a keen eye to follow it. London has her Palace and Tower, and her St. Stephen's Chapel; but the human race owes her no such memories. France has spots marked by the sublimest devotion; but the pilgrimage and the Mecca of the man who believes and hopes for the human race is not to Paris. It is to the seaboard cities of the great Republic. And when the flag was assailed, when the merchant waked up from his gain, the scholar from his studies, and the regiments marched one by one through the streets, which were the pavements that thrilled under their footsteps? What walls did they salute as the regimental flags floated by to Gettysburg and Antietam? These! Our boys carried down to the battle-fields the memory of State street and Faneuil Hall and the Old South Church.

We had a signal prominence in those early days. It was not our merit; it was an accident, perhaps. But it was a great accident in our favor that the British Parliament chose Boston as the first and prominent object of its wrath. It was on the men of Boston that Lord North visited his revenge. It was our port that was to be shut and its commerce annihilated. It was Sam Adams and John Hancock who enjoy the everlasting reward of being the only names excepted from the royal proclamation of forgiveness.

It was only an accident; but it was an accident which, in the stirring history of the most momentous change the world has seen, placed Boston in the van. Naturally, therefore, in our streets and neighborhood came the earliest collision between England and the Colonies. Here Sam Adams, the ablest and ripest statesman God gave to the epoch, forecast those measures which welded thirteen Colonies into one thunderbolt, and launched it at George the Third. Here Otis magnetized every boy into a desperate rebel. Here the fit successors of Knox and Hugh Peters consecrated their pulpits to the defence of that doctrine of the freedom and sacredness of man, which the State borrowed so directly from the Christian Church. The towers of the North Church rallied the farmers to the Lexington and Concord fights; and these old walls echoed the people's shout, when Adams brought them word that Gov. Hutchinson surrendered and withdrew the red coats. Lingering here still, are the echoes of those clashing sabres and jingling spurs that dreamt Warren could be awed to silence. Otis's blood immortalizes State street, just below where Attucks fell (our first martyr), and just above where zealous patriots made a teapot of the harbor.

It was a petty town, of some twenty thousand inhabitants; but "the rays of royal indignation collected upon it served only to illuminate, and could not consume." Almost every one of its houses had a legend. Every public building hid what was treasonable debate, or bore bullet-marks or bloodshed, — evidence of royal displeasure. It takes a stout heart to step out of a crowd and risk the chances of support, when failure is death. The strongest, proudest, most obstinate race and kingdom on one side: a petty town the assailant, — its weapons, ideas; its trust, God and the right; its old-fashioned men patiently arguing with cannon and regiments, blood the seal of the debate, and every stone and wall and roof and doorway witness forever of the angry tyrant and sturdy victim.

Now, gentlemen, man is not a mere animal, to eat and sleep and gain and lay up and enjoy, and pass away to his fathers. If we had been only that; if the North had been a peddler race, as the South supposed, not willing to risk sixpence for an idea, — no Democratic lawyers in yonder Court street would have shut up their doors, put their keys in their pockets, and asked of Gov. Andrew a commission, when that piece of bunting was fired upon near Fort Sumpter! It was only six feet square of cotton; it was only a few stars and stripes; it was only an insult offered to the sentiment of twenty millions of people. But it made Democrats and Republicans forget their differences, and a million of men crowd down to the Gulf. It was only a sentiment. But what does it feed on? Ascend one of those lofty buildings above Chicago, and grow weary in counting her crowd of masts and her miles of warehouses; and when you have done it, you remember that the sagacity and the thrift of three hundred thousand men have created that great centre of industry, and there comes to your mind perhaps sooner than anything else the old lullaby, —

> " How doth the little busy bee
> Improve each shining hour,
> And gather honey all the day
> From every opening flower!"

It is industry; it is thrift; it is comfort; it is wealth. But on Bunker Hill let somebody point out to you the church-tower whose lantern told Paul Revere that Middlesex was to be invaded. Search till your eye rests on this tiny spire, which trembled once when the mock Indian whoop bade England defiance. There is the elm where Washington first drew his sword. Here Winter Hill, whose cannon-ball struck Brattle-street Church. At your feet the sod is greener for the blood of Warren, which settled it forever that no more laws were to be made for us in London. The thrill you feel is that *sentiment* which, in 1862, made twenty million men, who had wrangled for forty years, close up their angry ranks, and carry that insulted bunting "to the Gulf," treading down dissensions and prejudices harder to conquer than Confederate cannon. We cannot afford to close any school which teaches such lessons.

Go ask the Londoner, crowded into small space, what number of pounds laid down on a square foot, what necessities of business, would induce him to pull down the Tower, and build a counting-house on its site! Go ask Paris what they will take from some business corporation for the spot where Mirabeau and Danton, or, later down, Lamartine saved the great flag of the tri-color from being drenched in the blood of their fellow-citizens! What makes Boston a history? Not so many men, not so much commerce. It is ideas. You might as well plough it with salt, and remove bodily into the more healthy elevation of Brookline or Dorchester, but for State street, Faneuil Hall, and the Old South!

What does *Boston* mean? Since 1630, the living fibre, running through history, which owns that name, means jealousy of power, unfettered speech, keen sense of justice, readiness to champion any good cause. That is the *Boston* Laud suspected, North hated, and the negro loved. If you destroy the scenes which perpetuate *that* Boston, then rebaptize her Cottonville or Shoetown. Don't belittle these memories! they lie long hid, but only to grow stronger. You mobbed John Brown meetings in 1860, and seemed to forget him in 1861; but the boys in blue, led by that very mob, wearing epaulets, marched from State street to the Gulf, because "John Brown's soul was marching on." That and the flag — only two memories, two *sentiments* — led the ranks.

My friend has told you that the church has removed its altar: we submit. God is not worshipped in temples builded with men's hands; and when their tower lifted itself in proud beauty to the heavens, and varied stone and rich woods furnished a new shelter for the descendants of Eckley and Prince and Sewall, and the others that worshipped here, the consecration that the Puritans gave these walls, — to Christ and the Church, — was annulled.

But these walls received as real a consecration when Adams and Otis dedicated them to liberty. We do not come here because there went hence to heaven the prayers of Sewall and Prince and the early saints of the colony. We come to save walls that heard and stirred the eloquence of Quincy — that keen blade which so soon wore out the scabbard — determined "under God, that wheresoever, whensoever, or howsoever we shall be called to make our exit, WE WILL DIE FREEMEN!" These arches will speak to us, as long as they stand, of the sublime and sturdy religious enthusiasm of Adams; of Otis's passionate eloquence and single-hearted devotion; of Warren in his young genius and enthusiasm; of a plain, unaffected, but high-souled people, who ventured all for a principle, and to transmit to us, unimpaired, the free lips and self-government which they inherited. Above and around us, unseen hands have written, "This is the cradle of Civil Liberty, child of earnest religious faith." I will not say it is a nobler consecration: I will not say that it is a better use. I only say we come here to save what our fathers consecrated to the memories of the most successful struggle the race has ever made for the liberties of man. You spend half a million for a schoolhouse. What school so eloquent as these walls to educate citizens? Napoleon turned his Simplon road aside to save a tree Cæsar had once mentioned. Won't you turn a street or spare a quarter of an acre to remind boys what sort of men their fathers were? Think twice before you touch these walls. We are only the world's trustees. The Old South no more belongs to us than Luther's or Hampden's, or Brutus's name does to Germany, England, or Rome. Each and all are held in trust as torchlight guides and inspiration for any man struggling for justice, and ready to die for the truth.

I went to Chicago more than twenty years ago; and they showed me the log house, thirty feet square and twenty feet high, in which the first officer of the United States, the first white man, lived, where now are half a million of human beings. There it nestled amid spacious inns, costly warehouses, and luxurious homes. I said to them, "Why not cover it with plate glass, let it stand there forever, the cradle of the great city of the lakes?" But I could not wake any sentiment in that quarter-million of traders; and the ancestral cabin which, to an anointed eye, measured the vast space between that 1816 and 1856, with its wealth and splendor, passed away. Then I came back here. That same week I found at my door a slaveholder from Arkansas. Singularly enough, in those bitter years, he trusted himself to me as a guide through the historic scenes of Boston. But it shows you how true it is that a prophet has no honor in his own household. How his reputation grows the farther off you get! Well, the first place I took him to was the house of John Hancock. We ascended those steps. I had learned from his talk, that, on that frontier where he was born, he had never seen a building older than twenty-five years. As we stood under that balcony, which some of you may remember, he turned to me, and said, "Is it actually true that the man who signed the Declaration of Independence stood on this flagstone, and lifted that latch?" I said, "Yes, sir; and above you, his body lay in state for some six or eight days." The man sat down on the flagstone wholly unnerved, his face pale with emotion. Said he, "You must excuse me; but I never felt as I feel to-day." That was Boston revealing to an every-day life the patriotism and nobleness smothered by petty cares. He came to our streets to wake that throb in his nature: he grew a better man and a more chivalrous citizen when that thrill answered to the memory of the first signer of the Declaration.

Gentlemen, these walls are the college for such training. The saving of this landmark is the best monument you can erect to the men of the Revolution. You spend $40,000 here, and $20,000 there, to put up a statue of some old hero: you want your son to gaze on the nearest approach to the features of those "dead but sceptred sovereigns who still rule our spirits from their urns." But what is a statue of Cicero compared to standing where your voice echoes from pillar and wall that actually heard his philippics! How much better than a picture of John Brown is the sight of that Blue Ridge which filled his eye, when, riding to the scaffold, he said calmly to his jailer, "This is a beautiful country: I never noticed it before." Destroy every portrait of Luther, if you must, but save that terrible chamber where he fought with the devil and translated the Bible. Scholars have grown old and blind, striving to put their hands on the very spot where bold men spoke, or brave men died. Shall we tear in pieces the roof that actually trembled to the words which made us a nation? It is impossible not to believe, if the spirits above us are permitted to know what passes in this terrestrial sphere, that Adams and Warren and Otis are to-day bending over us, asking that the scene of their immortal labors shall not be desecrated, or blotted from the sight of men.

Consecrate it again, in the worship and memory of a people! Consecrate it, in order that, if another rebellion breaks out against the flag; if our young men need once more to have their hearts quickened to the sublime significance of the Republic which protects them; if once more we must rally flags and marshal ranks for the protection of liberty, the young men shall be able to look up to Faneuil Hall and the Old State House and these walls as a quickening inspiration, before they leave these streets to go down and show themselves worthy of their fathers. Let these walls stand, if only to remind us that, in those days, Adams and Otis, advocates of the newest and extremest liberty, found their sturdiest allies in the pulpit; that our Revolution was so much a crusade that the Church led the van.

Summon it again, ye venerable walls, to its true place in the world's toil for good. Give us Mayhews and Coopers again, — and let the children of the Pilgrims show that religious conviction, veneration for "the great of old," and a stern purpose that our flag shall everywhere and always mean justice, are a threefold cord holding this nation together, never to be broken. We have a great future before us, — how grand, human forecast cannot measure, — yes, a great future, endangered by many and grave perils. Our way out of these faith believes in, but mortal eye cannot see. It is wisdom to summon every ally, to save every possible help. Educate the people to noble purpose. Lift them to the level of the highest motive. Enforce by every possible appeal the influence of the finest elements of our nature. Let the great ideas, — self-respect, freedom, justice, self-sacrifice, — help each man to tread the body under his feet. This worship of great memories, noble deeds, sacred places — the poetry of history — is one of the keenest ripeners of such elements. Seize greedily on every chance to save and emphasize these.

Give me a people freshly and tenderly alive to such influences, and I will laugh at money-rings or demagogues armed with sensual temptations. Men marvelled at the uprising which hurled slavery to the dust. It was young men who dreamed dreams over patriot graves — enthusiasts wrapped in memories! Marble, gold, and granite are not *real:* the only actual reality is an idea.

Gentlemen, I remember — Mr. Chairman, you will remember also — that some six months ago the Mayor and Aldermen debated how they should use some $18,000 or $20,000 left them by Jonathan Phillips to ornament the streets of Boston; and then the City Government decided — and decided very properly — that they could do no better with that money than place before the people a statue of the great mayor, Josiah Quincy, to whom this city owes so much. It was a very worthy vote under those circumstances; but if the great mayor were living to-day, he would be here with the Massachusetts ——. Yes, he would be here, Mr. Chairman, with the Massachusetts Historical Society in his right hand and the Mechanic Association in the other, and he would protest against the use of a dollar of that money for his personal honor until it had been first used to save this immortal legacy. I wish that I had a voice in that aldermanic corps, I would propose, with no discredit to the great mayor — let no one tear a leaf from his well-earned laurels! — but it was the mechanics of Boston that threw tea into the dock; it was the mechanics of Boston that held up the hands of Sam Adams; it was the mechanics of Boston, Paul Revere one of them, that made the Green Dragon immortal, — and I would take that $18,000 and add $50,000 more, and let the city preserve this building as a Mechanics' Exchange for all time. The merchants have their gilded room, fit gathering-place for consultations; but the men that carried us through the Revolution — caulkers! why, some men think we borrowed *caucus* from their name! — the men that carried us through the Revolution, were the mechanics of Boston. Where do they gather to-day? On the sidewalks and pavements of Court street, in the open air! We owe them a debt, in memory of what this grand movement, in its cradle, owed to them. I would ally the Green Dragon Tavern and the Sons of Liberty with the Old South, the grandsons and great-grandsons and representatives of the men who made the bulk of that meeting before which Hutchinson quailed, and Col. Dalrymple put on his hat and left the Council Chamber.

It was the message of the mechanics of Boston that Sam Adams carried to the Governor and to Congress. They sent him to Salem and Philadelphia: they lifted and held him up till even purblind George III. could distinguish his ablest opposer, and learned to hate with discrimination.

Shelter them under this roof: consecrate it in its original form to a grand public use for the common run of the people, — the bone and muscle. It will be the normal school of politics. It will be the best civil-service reform agency that the Republican party can adopt and use to-day.

The influence of these old walls will prevent men, if anything can, from becoming the tools of corruption or tyranny. "Recall every day one good thought — read one fine line," says the German Shakespeare. Yes, let every man's daily walk catch one ray of golden light, and his pulse throb once each day nobly, as he passes these walls! No gold, no greed, can canker the heart of such a people. Once in their hands, neither need, greed, nor the clamor for wider streets, will ever desecrate what Adams and Warren and Otis made sacred to the liberties of man!

www.ingramcontent.com/pod-product-compliance
Lightning Source LLC
LaVergne TN
LVHW020641110826
845149LV00004B/1311

9781418189891